T0046638

SUPER STEAM

10 FUN

EXPERIMENTS ABOUT ART AND MUSIC

BRING SCIENCE HOME

Published in 2024 by The Rosen Publishing Group, Inc.
2544 Clinton Street, Buffalo, NY 14224

Contains material from Scientific American , a division of Springer Nature America, Inc., reprinted by permission as well as original material from The Rosen Publishing Group.

Editor: Kristen Rajczak Nelson
Designer: Rachel Rising

All illustrations by Continuum Content Solutions

Activity on p. 5 by Science Buddies, Sabine De Brabandere (December 20, 2018); p. 11 by Science Buddies, Svenja Lohner (December 6, 2018); p. 17 by Science Buddies (June 18, 2015); p. 24 by Science Buddies (May 14, 2015); p. 30 by Science Buddies (November 13, 2014); p. 35 by Science Buddies (December 4, 2014); p. 40 by Science Buddies (August 28, 2014); p. 45 by Science Buddies (March 27, 2014); p. 49 by Science Buddies (January 30, 2014); p. 54 by Science Buddies (February 21, 2013).

Photo Credits: pp. 3, 4, 11, 15, 24, 28, 35, 38, 54, 58, 59 cve iv/Shutterstock.com; pp. 5, 11, 17, 24, 40, 35, 49, 45, 49, 50 Anna Frajtova/Shutterstock.com.

Names: Scientific American, Inc.
Title: Super STEAM: 10 fun experiments about art and music / edited by the Scientific American Editors.
Description: New York : Scientific American Educational Publishing, 2024. | Series: Bring science home | Includes glossary and index.
Identifiers: ISBN 9781725349278 (pbk.) | ISBN 9781725349285 (library bound) | ISBN 9781725349292 (ebook)
Subjects: LCSH: Science--Experiments--Juvenile literature. | Art and science--Juvenile literature. | Music and science--Juvenile literature.
Classification: LCC Q182.3 S88 2024 | DDC 507.8--dc23

Manufactured in the United States of America

Find us on

CONTENTS

✸ THESE ACTIVITIES INCLUDE
SCIENCE FAIR PROJECT IDEAS.

INTRODUCTION

Studying STEAM topics—science, technology, engineering, art, and math—is a great way to connect a love of the arts with an interest in how things work. In this book, you'll find experiments dealing with singing, video game design, and even tie-dye, each supplemented with the science that makes them happen. It's time to get creative, as well as scientific!

Projects marked with ⚛ include a section called Science Fair Project Ideas. These ideas can help you develop your own original science fair project. Science fair judges tend to reward creative thought and imagination, and it helps if you are really interested in your project. You will also need to follow the scientific method. See page 61 for more information about that.

The Science of Frescos

USE A LITTLE SCIENCE TO SEE HOW ARTISTS HAVE
CREATED MASTERPIECES FOR CENTURIES.

Have you ever wondered what art and science have in common? Although art draws on emotions and science uses rational thought, science and art both demand creativity and excellent observational skills. Most techniques used by artists even have interesting scientific explanations. This activity explores just one: painting with water-based paint on wet surfaces. See how science can help you become a more versatile artist!

PROJECT TIME
45 minutes

KEY CONCEPTS
Chemistry
Water
Saturation
Absorption

BACKGROUND

A fresco is a wall-painting technique that uses water-based paint on wet lime plaster. The technique is a marvelous work of chemistry—but it's not without risk! First, extreme heat above around 1,500°F (815°C) is applied to limestone, or $CaCO_3$, a sedimentary rock found in warm, shallow marine waters. This breaks the rock down into carbon dioxide—CO_2, the gas we exhale—and quicklime, or CaO. Quicklime, a toxic substance in itself, is then dissolved in water to create slaked lime, or $Ca(OH)_2$, a substance that can cause chemical burns. Microscopic particles, such as sand, are then mixed in to form the plaster used as a surface on which to paint.

These particles play an essential role because they create air pockets inside the mixture, which allows carbon dioxide to creep in and react with the slaked lime to form limestone—$CaCO_3$, the substance we started with! Before letting the plaster dry, painters apply water-based paint. This is a mixture of water and colorful particles called pigments that can be applied onto the wet plaster, which absorbs the water carrying the pigments. Then the water evaporates, the plaster sets, and the pigments become a part of the wall—a fresco is born!

Because the pigments penetrate into the plaster, frescos are durable. We can still see remnants of frescos made around 1500 BCE on the Greek island of Crete. Other great examples are found in the ruins of the ancient Roman city of Pompeii or in Italian Renaissance works, such as Michelangelo's frescos on the ceiling of the Sistine Chapel in Vatican City.

In this activity, you will investigate painting with water-based paint on wet surfaces. We will replace the toxic lime plaster used in traditional frescos with a homemade cornstarch mixture that is also fun to play with: oobleck.

MATERIALS

- Pie pan
- Measuring cup
- Cornstarch
- Water
- Measuring cup
- Liquid food coloring or watercolor paint (One color is enough to do the activity but several will yield a more colorful painting.)
- Small bowl to mix food coloring or paint with water (one for each color you use)
- Paintbrush (one for each color)
- Sheet of watercolor or construction paper (preferably a light color)
- Cloth or paper towels

Work surface where you can
use food coloring or paint

Sponge (optional)
Fork (optional)

PREPARATION •

- **Note:** Prepare to get messy and be careful not to get any oobleck or paint in your eyes. Always wash your hands after handling oobleck or paint.

- Slowly mix 2 cups of cornstarch with 1 cup (236 ml) of water in the pie pan. If you have a small pan, use half as much. You can use your hands or a fork for mixing. The result should be a gluelike mixture that slowly oozes between your fingers if you pick it up. Add small amounts of water if the substance seems too dry. This mixture is often called oobleck.

- Once you are done playing with the paste, leave it in the middle of the pan and let it sit for at least 15 minutes. Watch how it slowly oozes out and fills the pan.

- Mix a few drops of food coloring or watercolor paint with a bit of water in a small bowl. This is your water-based paint.

- Just before you start the activity let water run over the paper or wet it with a sponge so its surface is wet (but not soaked through).

PROCEDURE •

- In a moment you will paint two lines—one on the wet paste in the pie pan and the other on the wet paper. *Do you expect the lines to look sharp and crisp or soft and spread out?*

- Take a paintbrush, pick up some paint, and paint a line on the wet paper. *What happens? Why would this be?*

7

- Pick up some more paint and paint a line on the wet paste in the pie pan. *What happens now? Why would this look different?*

- Go ahead and paint whatever you feel like on the wet paste and on the wet paper. *Is the effect of the water-based paint on wet paper and on wet paste different? Why would this be?*

- Once you are done painting, let both paintings dry and observe the results. *Can you explain why these techniques create such different results?*

ExTRA

Use red cabbage juice instead of water to make the paste and to wet your paper. Use white vinegar and/or a mixture of baking soda and water as paint. *Do you see how these transparent paints create color? Can you find more substances in the house to paint on this cabbage juice-soaked base?*

ExTRA

Explore how water-based paint works on different types of dry and wet paper. *Is printer paper different from construction paper, watercolor paper, or cardboard? What happens if you first make all these types of paper wet? How can you combine both techniques?*

OBSERVATIONS AND RESULTS ·········

Were your lines soft and spread out on wet paper, and sharp and crisp on the wet paste? That is expected!

Even though the paste is wet, it is not saturated; it can absorb more water. As a result, the water-based paint penetrates the paste carrying the colorful pigments with it. This leaves a crisp, well-defined line on the surface.

Painting on wet paper is slightly different. The small air pockets between the paper fibers quickly fill with water. Once the paper is saturated, it can no longer absorb any more moisture. Water-based paint applied on a saturated surface floats on top of the paper, carrying the pigments with it. The result is a soft line with crinkly edges.

In both cases, the water evaporates, leaving the pigments as well as the cornstarch or paper behind.

CLEANUP

Wash all equipment (and any soiled work surface) with soapy water and wipe them clean. Discard the oobleck paste in the trash. Do not forget to wash your hands once you are done.

Make Marbled Cards Using Science!

MAKE YOUR OWN CARDS—WITH A LITTLE CHEMISTRY!

Are you in need of cards for family or friends? No problem—in this activity, you will create beautiful artwork and practice science at the same time! The only materials you need are shaving cream, food coloring, and sheets of paper. Ready to discover where the science is hiding? Go ahead and find out!

PROJECT TIME
30 minutes

KEY CONCEPTS
Chemistry
Solutions
Miscibility
Polarity
Surfactants
Surface tension

BACKGROUND

Paper marbling is an artistic method in which colors floating on a liquid surface are transferred onto paper to create a marbled pattern. The art of paper marbling dates back to the 10th century when Japanese artists developed a technique called suminagashi, which means "floating ink." Oil-based ink is dropped into a shallow pan of water where it floats on the surface. Paper is laid on top of the floating ink, and the color transfers to the paper's surface.

Another paper-marbling method that originated in Turkey and central Asia involves a thick liquid, called size, made from substances such as cornstarch. In this method, the liquid has to be thickened because the colors used are water-based and would otherwise not float. To make the colors float and spread even better, they are mixed with surfactants then dropped onto the size, which results in a pattern of floating color that can similarly be transferred onto paper.

This ancient art technique actually involves a lot of science! The colors float because they are less dense than water. It is also important that the colors and the water do not mix. Whether a liquid mixes with another depends on their individual molecular structures. The molecules that make up a liquid can be either polar or nonpolar. The simple rule "like dissolves like" says polar substances dissolve in polar liquids and nonpolar substances dissolve in nonpolar liquids. Water is polar whereas oil is nonpolar, which is why they don't mix.

Substances that dissolve in water are called hydrophilic; those that do not are hydrophobic. Surfactants are added to the colors to influence their spreading behavior. These special molecules can do this because they have two ends: one hydrophilic, the other hydrophobic. This property of surfactants allows substances to spread out better because it decreases water's surface tension, which results from water molecules holding together at the surface because they are slightly attracted to one another—more than they are to the air above.

In this activity you will do a simpler version of paper marbling using shaving cream and food coloring. It sounds different, but the same concepts apply. See for yourself and do this fun artistic science activity!

MATERIALS

- Two large plates
- Shaving cream (not gel)
- Liquid food coloring (at least two different colors)
- White paper or card stock
- Medical dropper
- Scissors
- Spoon

- Toothpick
- Jumbo craft stick
- Paper towels
- Spray bottle
- Water
- Workplace that can tolerate spills
- Adult helper (optional)
- Iron (optional)
- Vegetable oil (optional)
- Rubbing alcohol (optional)

PREPARATION ··

- Place the two plates next to each other on your workspace.

- Cut two letter-size pieces of paper in half crosswise. Then fold each in half, creating two folded cards.

- Put water in the spray bottle, and set it aside.

PROCEDURE ·······································

- Put shaving cream on the two plates, and spread it out with your hands or a spoon to create a layer with an area at least as large as your paper card and a depth of about 1/2 inch (1.3 cm). *How does the shaving cream feel? More like a liquid or a solid?*

- Take the first color of your food coloring and add several drops on top of the shaving cream using a medical dropper or dripping it straight from the bottle. Do this with both plates. *What happens to the color once it drops on top of the shaving cream? Does it mix with the foam, sink into it, or stay on top?*

- Repeat with all other food colors you want to use. *Do all the colors behave the same way? Can you see a color pattern develop on the foam's surface?*

13

Next, take the toothpick and carefully swirl around the color in the shaving cream until you have created a color pattern that you like. Try not to overmix the colors. *What happens when you swirl the colors around? Do they mix with the shaving cream or do they stay separate?*

Use the spray bottle to spray some water on top of the color pattern on one of the plates. Use at least five to 10 pumps of water. Then let the foam sit for about one minute. *Does the color pattern look different once you have sprayed the water on top? How does it differ from the color pattern on the other plate?*

Place your first card with the front side facing down on top of the shaving cream and press it lightly so that the whole card is covered by the shaving cream.

Repeat with the second card and the second plate.

Carefully remove both cards from the shaving cream, turn them around, and scrape the remaining cream from the cards' surfaces with the craft stick. *What do you see on the paper once the shaving cream is removed? Do you notice a difference between the two cards? Can you explain your results?*

Let the cards dry. If the paper wrinkles, you can ask an adult to carefully iron it at the lowest heat setting and another sheet of paper between your card and the iron.

ExTRA

Try to play around with more colors, different swirl patterns, and varying sizes of paper. *How many different patterns can you create?*

SCIENCE FAIR IDEA

What happens if you spray oil or rubbing alcohol instead of water on top of your color pattern? Will your results differ? Get some vegetable oil and rubbing alcohol to find out!

OBSERVATIONS AND RESULTS ·········

Were you able to make beautiful, marbled paper cards? This method works very similarly to the others described in the beginning. Shaving cream is made of a mixture of soap and water with a gas that can turn liquid into foam when you spray it out of the bottle. Soap is a surfactant, which means its molecule has a hydrophilic (water-loving) and hydrophobic (water-repelling) end. Liquid food coloring is a mixture of dye in water or alcohol and is hydrophilic. When you drop the food coloring on the shaving cream, it won't soak in because it can only interact with the hydrophilic parts of the soap molecules and is repelled by the hydrophobic ends. Even if you swirl the colors with a toothpick, you still see a distinct separation between the color and the shaving cream.

When you put the paper on top of the color pattern, the food dye gets soaked into the paper, transferring the whole pattern onto its surface. This is because paper is made from wood pulp, which mainly consists of cellulose found in the cell walls of green plants—a hydrophilic molecule. The hydrophilic food dye can spread easily across the paper, creating a beautiful marbled pattern. When you spray water on top of your pattern before you put the paper on top, however, the food dye mixes with the water and is carried into the deeper layers of the foam. You might have noticed your color pattern looked washed out after adding the water. The pattern on the paper does look much fainter than the other one—but it is just as beautiful!

CLEANUP ··························

Use paper towels to remove the shaving cream from the plates, then dispose of everything in the trash. After you rinse the plates with hot water and soap, you can reuse them. Don't throw away your cards—you might want to send them to family and friends!

15

Compelling Compositions
Do Photography Masters Follow Rules?

WHAT HELPS MAKE A GOOD PICTURE? TRY THIS
ACTIVITY, AND YOU'LL FIND OUT HOW TO TAKE
BETTER PHOTOS YOURSELF—IN A SNAP!

PROJECT TIME
45 minutes

KEY CONCEPTS
Art
Visual perception
Photography
Composition

Do you like to preserve a moment with a photo or tell a story with pictures? It can feel very rewarding to capture an experience in a compelling photo; it can also be disappointing when the image does not convey what you were seeing or what you had in mind. You might wonder what makes some photos mesmerizing and gripping, whereas others look dull, empty, or less appealing. It might be easier than you think to create those effective photographs. Some easy composition rules, such as the "rule of thirds" and the "golden mean" have been around for centuries. Do compelling photos follow these rules or does it take more than rules to create an impressive composition? Could applying these rules improve your photography? Do other art forms, such as drawing or painting, follow similar rules? In this science activity, you will browse through some famous works of photographic art and investigate how often these follow some basic rules of composition.

17

BACKGROUND

Photography classes provide students with some easy-to-follow rules on composition to help them create visually interesting photos. One of the most popular rules is the rule of thirds. To apply this rule, look through the viewfinder of your camera, divide the image frame into thirds—both horizontally and vertically—and place the important elements you want to capture either along these lines or where the lines intersect. Some cameras even show these horizontal and vertical "thirds" lines in the viewfinder.

A less famous but still practical rule of composition is referred to as the golden mean. This rule puts more emphasis on the diagonal. To use this rule, mentally imagine a diagonal line drawn from one corner of the frame to the opposite corner and that two dots divide that diagonal line into three equal parts. Then connect these points to the remaining corners of the frame. Here again, you place the main elements along these lines or at the intersection of these lines (the dots).

Now that you know two main concepts for composition, you are ready to look at some published photos and investigate whether or not these follow some of the photography rules—and in what cases good photographs might stray from the rules.

MATERIALS

- A photo book (Preferably use one that includes work by many different photographers using different styles; or if you would like to focus on a particular photographer, you can use a book of their collective work. You could also choose a particular theme, such as nature pictures or close-ups. If you cannot find a photo book, try magazine photos or a picture book, such as those by Mo Willems.)
- Two different-colored permanent markers
- Two transparency films or clear sheet protectors
- A ruler
- Paper and pen

- Select a photo size that you would like to focus on. It should be smaller than the size of your transparencies and occur frequently in your book or in your selected photos.

- Use a permanent marker to draw the outline or frame of a photo with the selected size on the film.

- Draw two parallel, horizontal lines within your outline, such that they divide the frame in three equal horizontal strips. These lines will be used to test if the photo follows the horizontal rule of thirds.

- Add two equidistant, vertical lines to your outline, dividing the frame vertically in three equal strips. These vertical lines will be used to test if the photo follows the vertical rule of thirds.

- With a different-colored permanent marker, color the dots where the horizontal and vertical lines you just drew intersect. These dots will be used to test if the main elements are placed on one or more intersections of the vertical and horizontal thirds lines. This completes the template to test the rule of thirds.

- Now use a permanent marker to make a golden mean template on a different transparency film. First draw the outline or frame of a photo with the selected size on the film.

- Draw one diagonal line by connecting one corner of the outline with the opposite corner. *Why do you think you need only one diagonal line? Rotate your frame; does that make a difference? Now flip it; does that make a difference?*

- Find the two points on the diagonal line that divide the diagonal line's length in three equal parts. Mark these points as dots with a different-colored permanent marker.

- Using the first color of permanent marker, connect the dots you just drew, each to the closest remaining corner of the frame. This completes the template to test the golden mean rule.

- Create a table in which to record your observations: Using a piece of paper, make a column for the following five categories: Horizontal Rule of Thirds; Vertical Rule of Thirds; Horizontal and Vertical Rule of Thirds; Golden Mean; No Rule.

PROCEDURE

Browse through the photo book. For each photo that is the size of your template frame, see if you can guess which rule it might follow. *Are there strong horizontal or vertical lines present in the image that are approximately at one-third of the frame's horizontal or vertical size? Is the main subject placed on a horizontal third, a vertical third, or on an intersection of both third lines?* If so, the photo probably follows the rule of thirds. To see if the golden mean rule is used, look for a strong diagonal line. *Is the main subject placed at one-third sections of the length of this diagonal line?*

In the next steps, you will classify each photo you analyze in one of the columns of your data table. Be sure to make clear references to your photos; you might want to come back to one of them later. A clear reference might include the page number in the book, the title, the date on which it was taken, and the photographer.

Lay the rule of thirds template over the photo. *Is there a clear indication that the image follows the horizontal rule of thirds, the vertical rule of thirds, or maybe both?* Note that it is enough if one strong horizontal or vertical third line is present to classify it as following the horizontal or vertical rule of thirds. If a main element in the photo is placed at an intersection of third lines, classify it as following both the horizontal and vertical rule of thirds. If you found that this picture follows a rule of thirds, note it in the appropriate column of your data table. Once a photo is classified, you can skip the next two steps and go to the next image.

- Lay the golden mean template over the photo. *Does it match this template, indicating that the image follows the golden mean rule?* Do not forget you can flip this template to see if the diagonal matches in the other direction. If you found a match, note the photo down in the golden mean column of your data table. If you classified this photo, skip the next step and instantly go to the next one.

- If you conclude this photo did not follow one of the basic composition rules, classify it in the "No Rule" column of your data table.

- Look at more photographs, analyzing and classifying them as you go. Collect as much data as possible. More data will give you a more accurate idea of whether or not published photos follow one or more of the basic composition rules.

- Once you feel you have gathered enough data, count the number of photos listed in each column of your table and write the total at the end of the column. *Do your numbers show a clear pattern? Is one type of rule more common than another?*

- Add up the totals for all four columns, indicating a basic composition rule was followed. *How does this total compare with the total number of photos you classified as not following a rule? What would you conclude? Are these rules strong ones that need to be followed to make a compelling image or are they really just guidelines, helpful hints that can create balanced compositions?* Maybe your data indicates that photos are creations of art that do not follow any rule.

ExTRA

Make a bar graph or pie chart showing the total number of photos you classified as following a rule versus the number not following a rule. *Do you find it easier to draw conclusions from the visual representation than from a number comparison? Would you be able to guess which fraction of all the photos you analyzed follow/do not follow a rule from the graphical representation?* You can also make a bar graph or pie chart of the number of pictures that follow each different type of composition rule. *Do you find this visual representation easier to understand or faster to read than the list of numbers?*

EXTRA

Use a camera and try some of these rules for yourself. *Do you think using one of these rules will change the way your photographs look?* You can also use a photo-editing program and reframe your photos digitally using the crop function. *Does following a composition rule make your images more expressive, more pleasing to the eye and more balanced?*

EXTRA

This activity focuses on the main elements in the photos. Photographers can use different compositions for the background, the foreground, and the subject of the picture. *Can you find these composition rules applied to different subsections of some images?*

EXTRA

Study whether or not these rules are more often followed in particular styles of photos. *Do you think these rules are equally effective for different types of images such as landscapes, portraits, close-ups, or action shots?*

EXTRA

The rule of thirds and the golden mean are well known in photography. *Do you think other art forms use these rules to create balanced and pleasing compositions?* Find out by browsing through some websites, picture books, paintings, or drawings. You can even look at sculptures, architecture, or objects in nature.

OBSERVATIONS AND RESULTS · · · · · · · · ·

Did you find photos following one of the basic composition rules and others not following any of them?

Proportion is an important element in composition, and an excellent tool to help create balanced, appealing photos. But it is not the only one; shape, texture, and color are just a few other elements to consider. Knowing this, you can see the rule of thirds and golden mean, although handy guidelines, aren't unbreakable rules. It is always up to the photographer to decide what works for a particular case.

You might have noticed that these basic composition rules work very well in some types of photos, such as action shots and landscapes. These rules often do not work as well in other areas. Close-ups or photos where symmetry is important often work better with the subject placed in the center and often don't follow the same composition rules.

More advanced photographers might use a composition rule based on the golden ratio to lead the eye and create visually pleasing compositions. The golden ratio and golden spiral can be seen in many art forms, and even in nature—like the whorls of a shell. Search further and see if you can find the golden ratio in famous pictures or in other art forms.

CLEANUP · · · · · · · · · · · · · ·

Dispose of your transparencies. Put away all other materials you used.

23

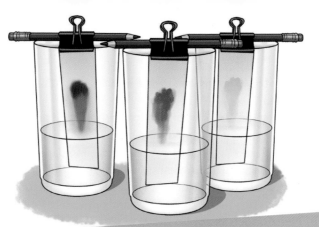

Chromatography
Be a Color Detective

INVESTIGATE THE MANY HUES OF A COLOR AND MORE IN THIS COLORFUL PROJECT.

PROJECT TIME

30 minutes

KEY CONCEPTS

Colors
Solutions
Molecules
Chromatography
Primary colors

Do you love to use bright and vibrant colored art supplies such as markers or paints? Do you ever wonder how these colors are made? The variety of colors comes from colored molecules. These are mixed into the material—whether ink or paint—to make the product. Some colored molecules are synthetic (or human-made), such as "Yellow No. 5" found in some food dyes. Others are extracted from natural sources, such as carotenoid (pronounced kuh-RAH-tuh-noid) molecules. These are molecules that make your carrot orange. They can be extracted from concentrated natural products, such as saffron. But there is more to making a color look the way it does in your homemade artwork. You might have learned that many colors, such as orange and green, are made by blending other, "primary" colors. So even though our eyes see a single color, the color of a marker, for instance, might be the result of one type of color molecule or it might be a mix of color molecules responsible. This science activity will help you discover the hidden colors in water-soluble markers.

24

BACKGROUND

We see objects because they reflect light into our eyes. Some molecules only reflect specific colors; it is this reflected, colored light that reaches our eyes and tells our brains that we are seeing a certain color.

Often the colors that we see are a combination of the light reflected by a mixture of different-color molecules. Even though our brains perceive the result as one color, each of the separate types of color molecules stays true to its own color in the mixture. One way to see this is to find a way to separate out the individual types of color molecules from the mixture—to reveal their unique colors.

Paper chromatography is a method used by chemists to separate the constituents (or parts) of a solution. The components of the solution start out in one place on a strip of special paper. A solvent (such as water, oil, or isopropyl alcohol) is allowed to absorb up the paper strip. As it does so, it takes part of the mixture with it. Different molecules run up the paper at different rates. As a result, components of the solution separate and, in this case, become visible as strips of color on the chromatography paper. Will your marker ink show different colors as you put it to the test?

MATERIALS

- Two white coffee filters
- Scissors
- Ruler
- Drawing markers (not permanent): brown, yellow, and any other colors you would like to test
- At least two pencils (one for each color you will be testing)
- At least two tall water glasses (one for each color you will be testing), 4 inches (10 cm) or taller
- Water
- Two binder clips or clothespins
- Drying rack or at least two additional tall water glasses (one for each color you will be testing)
- Pencil or pen and paper for taking notes

PREPARATION

- Carefully cut the coffee filters into strips that are each about 1 inch (2.5 cm) wide and at least 4 inches (10 cm) long. Cut at least two strips, one to test brown and one to test yellow. Cut an extra strip for each additional color you would like to test. *How do you expect each of the different colors to behave when you test it with the paper strip?*

- Draw a pencil line across the width of each paper strip, about 0.4 inch (1 cm) from the bottom end.

- Take the brown marker and a paper strip and draw a short line (about 0.4 inch [1 cm]) on the middle section of the pencil line. Your marker line should not touch the sides of your strip.

- Use a pencil to write the color of the marker you just used on the top end of the strip. Note: Do not use the colored marker or pen to write on the strips, as the color or ink will run during the test.

- Repeat the previous three steps with a yellow marker and then all the additional colors you would like to test.

- Hold a paper strip next to one of the tall glasses (on the outside of it), aligning the top of the strip with the rim of the glass, then slowly add water to the glass until the level just reaches the bottom end of the paper strip. Repeat with the other glass(es), keeping the strips still on the outside and away from the water. *What role do you think the water will play?*

PROCEDURE

Fasten the top of a strip (the side farthest from the marker line) to the pencil with a binder clip or clothespin. Pause for a moment. *Do you expect this color to be the result of a mixture of colors or the result of one color molecule?* If you like, you can make a note of your prediction now.

- Hang the strip in one of the glasses that is partially filled with water by letting the pencil rest on the glass rim. The bottom end of the strip should just touch the water level. If needed, add water to the glass until it is just touching the paper. **Note**: It is important that the water level stays below the marker line on the strip.

- Leave the first strip in its glass as you repeat the previous two steps with the second strip and the second glass. Repeat with any additional colors you are testing.

- Watch as the water rises up the strips. *What happens to the colored lines on the strips? Does the color run up as well? Do you see any color separation?*

- When the water level reaches about 0.4 inch (1 cm) from the top (this may take up to 10 minutes), remove the pencils with the strips attached from the glasses. If you let the strips run too long, the water can reach the top of the strips and distort your results.

- Write down your observations. *Did the colors run? Did they separate in different colors? Which colors can you detect? Which colors are on the top (meaning they ran quickly) and which are on the bottom (meaning they ran more slowly)?*

- Hang your strips to dry in the empty glasses or on a drying rack. Note that some colors might keep running after you remove the strips from the water. You might need longer strips to see the full spectrum of these colors. The notes you took in the previous step will help you remember what you could see in case the colors run off the paper strip. Look at your strips. *How many color components does each marker color have? Can you identify which colors are the result of a mixture of color components and which ones are the result of one hue of color molecule? Are individual color components brightly colored or dull in color? How many different colors can you detect in total?*

⚛ SCIENCE FAIR IDEA ∼∼∼∼

Most watercolor marker inks are colored with synthetic color molecules. Artists often like to work with natural dyes. It is fairly easy to make your own dye from colorful plants such as blueberries, red beets, or turmeric. To make your own dye, have an adult help you finely chop the plant material and place it in a saucepan. Add just enough water to cover the plant material. Let the mixture simmer covered on the stove for approximately 10 to 15 minutes. If, at this point, the color of your liquid is too faint, you might want to remove the lid of the saucepan and continue boiling until some liquid has evaporated and a more concentrated color is obtained. Let it cool and strain when needed. Now you have natural dye. (Handle with caution, as it can stain surfaces and materials.) To investigate the color components of this dye, repeat the previous procedure but replace the marker line with a drop of natural dye. A dropper will help create a nice drop. Let the drop of dye dry before running the paper strip. *Would the color of your natural dye be the result of a mixture of color molecules or one specific color molecule? Does the marker of the same color as your natural dye run in a similar way as your natural dye does?*

ExTRA ∼∼∼∼∼∼∼

In this activity, you used water-soluble markers in combination with water as a solvent. You can test permanent markers using isopropyl rubbing alcohol as a solvent. *Do you think similar combinations of color molecules are used to color similar-colored permanent markers?*

ExTRA ∼∼∼∼∼∼

You can investigate other art supplies, including paints, pastels, or inks in a similar way. Be sure to always choose a solvent that dissolves the material that is being tested to run the chromatography test. Isopropyl rubbing alcohol, vegetable oil, and salt water are some examples of solvents used to perform paper chromatography tests for different substances.

OBSERVATIONS AND RESULTS ·········

Did you find that brown is made up of several types of color molecules, whereas yellow only showed a single yellow color band?

Marker companies combine a small subset of color molecules to make a wide range of colors, much like you can mix paints to make different colors. But nature provides an even wider range of color molecules and also mixes them in interesting ways. As an example, natural yellow color in turmeric is the result of several curcuminoid molecules. The brown pigment umber (obtained from a dark brown clay) is caused by the combination of two color molecules: iron oxides (which have a rusty red-brown color) and manganese oxides (which add a darker black-brown color).

In this activity, you investigated the color components using coffee filters as chromatography paper. Your color bands might be quite wide and artistic, whereas scientific chromatography paper would yield narrow bands and more exact results.

CLEANUP ·······················

Throw away the paper strips and wash the glasses.

Sonorous Science
Making Music with Bottles

PUT MUSIC AND PHYSICS TOGETHER
IN THIS MELODIOUS PROJECT!

Have you ever blown across a bottle's top and made a pleasant, resonant sound? If so, have you wondered exactly how that note is made? A bottle is actually what is called a "closed-end air column." Clarinets and some organ pipes are examples of musical instruments that work in the same way. In this science activity, you will use bottles to investigate how the length of a closed-end air column affects the pitch of the note that it makes.

PROJECT TIME
20 minutes

KEY CONCEPTS
Music
Sounds
Physics
Sound waves

BACKGROUND

Some musical instruments produce sound from vibrating strings, others from vibrating reeds, and still others from resonating columns of air. In this activity, you'll try a simple example of the latter type of instrument: narrow-necked bottles that are partially filled with water. These bottles will function as closed-end air columns, which are basically tubes that are open at one end but closed (or covered) at the other.

How do musical instruments make the sounds that they do? All sound is made by vibrations that travel through the air. Specifically, these vibrations cause patterns of air compression that travel as a wave, with air pressure increases being followed by decreases. This is how sound itself is a wave. The pitch of the sound we hear depends on the frequency of the wave—how quickly an increase in air pressure is followed by a decrease. Higher pitches have higher frequencies.

MATERIALS

- Three identical narrow-neck bottles (They can be glass or plastic.)
- Permanent marker
- Ruler
- Water

PREPARATION

- Make sure the bottles are clean and empty.

- Try blowing across the tops of the bottles you selected to make a resonant sound. Do this by holding the bottle upright (so it is perpendicular to your face). Touch your lower lip to the edge of the bottle, pursing your upper lip, and blowing gently over the opening. When you get the angle and airflow just right, you will hear a musical note as the air column in the open bottle resonates. *How does the bottle sound?* If you cannot make a note by blowing over the bottles, try using different bottles for this activity.

31

PROCEDURE

- Measure the height of one of the bottles. Using the permanent marker and ruler, make a small mark at exactly halfway up the bottle. Fill this bottle with water up to the mark you made.

- On another bottle, make a small mark at exactly three-quarters up. Fill this bottle with water up to the mark you just made.

- Leave the third bottle empty.

- Blow across the top of the empty bottle, as you did before. Make sure you can make a clear note. Then blow across the top of the half-full bottle. *How does the note that the half-full bottle makes compare with that made by the empty bottle? Is the note from the half-full bottle higher or lower in pitch?*

- Then blow across the top of the bottle that is three-quarters full. It may take some practice to make a note from this bottle. *How does the note this bottle makes compare with the one made by the half-full bottle? Is it higher or lower in pitch than the half-full bottle?*

- *Overall, how do the notes made from the three bottles compare with one another? Why do you think that is?*

ExTRA

If you have a piano, electronic keyboard, or other musical instrument (or an electronic tuner), you could try comparing the notes from the bottles with the notes on a real instrument. Alternatively, you could try slowly filling a bottle with water, checking what notes it makes as it becomes fuller, and compare those with a real instrument. *What notes does it sound like the bottles are making? Can you figure out a relationship between the three notes from the bottles used in this activity?*

OBSERVATIONS AND RESULTS

Did the empty bottle produce the lowest pitch? Did the bottle that was filled three-quarters full with water make the highest pitch?

When playing a musical instrument that is a closed-end air column, such as the bottles in this activity, the pitch of the note that is made depends on the length of the air column. In other words, the pitch depends on how much water has filled up the bottle and how much empty space remains. This is because the pitch of the sound we hear depends on the frequency of the sound wave that can be created within the bottle's air. The shorter the air column (that is, the shorter the height of the air in the bottle) the higher the frequency. And the higher the frequency, the higher the perceived pitch. This is why the empty bottle should have produced a sound wave with a lower frequency than the others and the bottle that was nearly full (three-quarters full) should have made the highest pitch.

In fact, because the air column in the half-full bottle was half the length of the air column in the empty bottle, the half-full bottle should have produced a frequency twice the empty bottle's frequency. Similarly, the three-quarter-full bottle should have produced a frequency that was twice that of the half-full bottle. When one sound wave is twice the frequency of another, the pitches made are one octave apart. (For example, the middle C note on a piano has a frequency of 262 hertz whereas the C that is one octave higher has a frequency of 524 hertz.) This means that the half-full bottle should have made a note one octave higher than the empty bottle, and the three-quarter-full bottle should have made a note one octave higher than the half-full one.

CLEANUP

Recycle the bottles used. Put away any other materials where you found them.

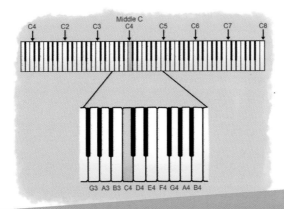

Singing Science
How High and Low Can You Go?

EXPLORE HOW VOICES WORK IN THIS
SONOROUS SCIENCE PROJECT!

Do you enjoy singing in a choir at school—or with friends or family? Singing can be a fun thing to do any time of the year! But have you noticed that different people tend to sing different parts of a song—or sing in different octaves? Have you ever wondered what the highest note is that you can sing? How about the lowest? Do you think males and females can reach most of the same notes? How about children and adults? In this "note"-worthy science activity, you'll get to answer some of these questions!

PROJECT TIME
1 hour

KEY CONCEPTS
Music
Singing
Pitch
Age
Gender

35

BACKGROUND

Have you ever started singing a song, and then realized a little way into the melody that the notes were too high or too low for you to sing well? If so, the song was outside of your vocal range. A person's vocal range consists of all the notes between the lowest and highest notes a person can comfortably sing.

To understand what might determine a person's vocal range, it is important to first understand what is happening when a person sings. When air is expelled from a person's lungs, it's carried out of the body through a tube called the trachea (or windpipe) in the throat. In the trachea, the air passes through the larynx (or voice box), which contains folds of tissue called the vocal cords. The vocal cords vibrate as air passes by them, and this vibration creates sound. If you place your fingers at the base of your throat as you sing or talk, you might be able to faintly feel these vibrations.

The pitch of the sound a person makes is determined by several factors, including the size and tension of their vocal cords. By changing some factors, people can produce different pitches, or notes.

MATERIALS

- Piano, keyboard, or a virtual piano online
- Volunteers (at least three). If you want to compare how age affects vocal range, you will want some adults aged 21 or older and some children aged 9 or younger (all of the same gender to make comparisons easier).

If you want to investigate how gender affects vocal range, be sure to include both males and females (all of the same age range).

36

PREPARATION

- Make sure you are familiar with the names and locations of the notes on the piano. Specifically, make sure you can find Middle C. Middle C is often called C4 because it is the fourth C key on a standard piano. If you do not know which key is Middle C (C4), you will need somebody who can show you or you can look for a diagram online that has labeled keys. *Can you find Middle C?*

- There are seven notes on a piano keyboard (A, B, C, D, E, F and G) that are repeated. The white keys on the piano represent these notes. *Can you identify these notes on the piano?* (The black keys are smaller shifts in pitch, either sharps or flats, and will not be used in this activity.)

- Familiarize yourself with the other notes on the keyboard. The keys to the right of C4 are higher in pitch. The D to the right of C4 is called D4, the D to the right of C5 (the fifth C key on a standard piano) is called D5, and so on. The keys to the left of C4 are lower in pitch. The B to the left of C4 is called B3, the B to the left of C3 is called B2, and so on. *Can you identify C3, C4, and C5, and the notes in between these ones?*

PROCEDURE

- Get your first volunteer ready, and play C4 on the piano, keyboard, or virtual piano keyboard. *Can the volunteer sing the note back to you?* If the volunteer can comfortably sing the note, then it is in their vocal range. (For this activity to accurately map vocal ranges, the volunteer has to actually sound like he or she is singing; if the "singing" sounds like grunting, growling, screeching, or squeaking, then it does not count and the note is not in the volunteer's vocal range.)

If the volunteer can sing C4, keep playing increasingly higher notes (to the right of C4) and have the volunteer sing them back until you reach a note that is no longer comfortable for them to sing. If the volunteer finds it helpful, they can sing "do," "re," "mi," "fa," "so," "la," "ti," "do," when singing increasingly higher-pitched notes (such as for singing the notes C4, D4, E4, F4, G4, A4, B4, and then C5). *What is the highest-pitched note that the volunteer can sing?* (This is the top of the volunteer's vocal range.)

To find the bottom of the volunteer's vocal range, go back to C4 and keep playing increasingly lower-pitched notes (to the left of C4) and have the volunteer sing each note back to you until you come to a note that is no longer comfortable for them to sing. If the volunteer finds it helpful, they can sing "do," "ti," "la," "so," "fa," "mi," "re," "do," when singing increasingly lower-pitched notes (such as for singing the notes C4, B3, A3, G3, F3, E3, D3, and then C3). *What is the lowest-pitched note that the volunteer can sing?* (This is the bottom of the volunteer's vocal range.)

Repeat this process with each of the other volunteers. *What is the vocal range for each volunteer?*

How do the vocal ranges of male and female children compare? What about male and female adults, and adults compared to children?

⚛ SCIENCE FAIR IDEA ∼∼∼

You could do this activity again but this time use at least 20 volunteers as follows: 10 adults (age 21 or older, including five males and five females) and 10 children (age 9 or younger, including five males and five females). *How does age and gender appear to affect a person's vocal range?*

OBSERVATIONS AND RESULTS ·········

Did you find that children typically have the highest vocal ranges (regardless of gender), and adult men typically have the lowest?

One thing a person cannot control is the length of their vocal cords, which affects the pitch of sound a person makes when singing. Vocal cord size is similar in young males and young females, which is why children—boys and girls—have a similar vocal range. (This is from about A3 to G5.) But as children go through puberty, their vocal cords grow longer, giving adults typically lower vocal ranges than children. By the time they're adults, most females have vocal cords that are between 0.5 and 0.7 inches (12.5 and 17.5 mm) long; adult males usually have longer vocal cords, between 0.6 and 1 inches (17 and 25 mm) in length. Consequently, singing voices for women are usually a little higher than for men, with the highest female voice (soprano) reaching C6 and the lowest one (contralto) going down to E3, while the highest male voice (countertenor, typically in falsetto) may hit E5, and the lowest one (bass) can drop down to E2.

CLEANUP ·········

There is no cleanup for this activity. But remember to thank your volunteers!

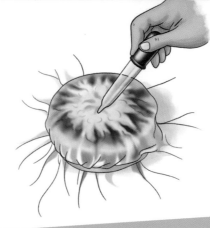

Soluble Science
Making Tie-Dye T-Shirts with Permanent Markers

ENJOY COLOR AND CHEMISTRY WHILE
GETTING CREATIVE IN THIS ACTIVITY.

Have you ever made a tie-dyed T-shirt? It can be a lot of fun to dye a shirt in bright colors with spiraling designs. In this science activity, you will get to dye a T-shirt with your own colorful artwork using only permanent markers. Along the way, you'll find out how solubility helps your drawings leave beautiful designs on the fabric.

PROJECT TIME
30 minutes

KEY CONCEPTS
Chemistry
Solubility
Solutions
Inks
Dyes

BACKGROUND

You've probably noticed that when a drop of water lands on a piece of paper with words or a picture printed on it, sometimes the ink runs. When this happens, the drop of water is at least partially absorbed into the paper and then flows through it. As the water moves, it carries the ink particles along with it. Why does the water move the ink? This is because of solubility—the ink has combined with the water.

Solubility is an important property of matter. If a chemical is soluble in water, then the chemical will dissolve, or appear to disappear, when it's added to water—or vice versa. This is why the ink can dissolve in the drop of water on the paper and then travel along with the water through the paper.

If a chemical is not soluble, also known as insoluble, then it will not dissolve. Can you think of some things that are insoluble in water? If a piece of paper were printed with ink that was insoluble in water, what would happen when a drop of water fell on it? The ink should remain in place on the paper and would not be carried away by the water flowing through the paper.

MATERIALS

- At least two rubber bands
- At least two plastic cups
- Colorful assortment of permanent markers
- Water
- 70 percent isopropyl alcohol (aka rubbing alcohol)
- Medicine dropper
- White T-shirt that can be dyed
- Newspapers (optional) (This is to protect your work surface.)
- Hair dryer (optional)

PREPARATION

- If you want to protect the surface on which you will be dyeing your T-shirt, cover it with a few layers of newspaper sheets. Note that permanent markers can stain fabric and other materials, so be careful when using them.

PROCEDURE

- Lay out the T-shirt on the surface where you will be dyeing it.

- Wherever you want to make a design on the T-shirt, place a plastic cup underneath the shirt (which should be flat so that both layers of the shirt are stretched over the cup) and then loop a rubber band around the edge of the cup, going from the front of the T-shirt. This should end up making a flat, tight circle of the shirt fabric stretched over the cup opening. Do this to at least two places on the T-shirt so that you have at least two flat circles in which to draw.

- Use the permanent markers to draw some colorful designs in each flat T-shirt circle that you made with the cups. Fill in at least two flat circles with your drawings.

- Use the medicine dropper to drop a few drops of water onto the center of one of the flat circles that you drew in. *What happens to the permanent marker ink when the water touches it?*

- Drop several more drops of water onto the same flat circle until it is thoroughly damp. *Does the permanent marker ink change as the piece of fabric becomes damp?*

- Now use the medicine dropper to drop a few drops of isopropyl alcohol onto the center of one of the other flat circles that you drew in. *What happens to the permanent marker ink when the alcohol touches it?*

- Drop several more drops of alcohol onto the same flat circle until it is thoroughly damp. *Does the permanent marker ink change as the piece of fabric becomes damp with alcohol?*

- Compare the two flat circles. *Which one looks better? Why do you think that might be?*

- **Tip:** If you want to make one of the flat circles look better, try letting it dry—either naturally or with a hairdryer—and then adding drops of the other liquid—water or alcohol—which should be the liquid that gave you the best results.

- If you want to make more colorful designs on your T-shirt, let the first ones dry and then repeat the procedure on different parts of the shirt where you want some artwork, but this time just use the liquid (water or alcohol) that gave you the best results!

ExTRA

To more closely compare results between using water versus alcohol, make a symmetrical design in one of the flat T-shirt circles and treat one half with water and the other half with alcohol. *How exactly does the one half of the circle look compared with the other half?*

ExTRA

If you wash the T-shirt made in this activity, you will probably find that the colors fade. *Can you figure out a way to keep the designs from fading?*

ExTRA

Some markers are made using multiple dyes, and you can see these dyes using a chemistry technique called chromatography. *Can you separate different dyes that are in permanent markers using chromatography?*

OBSERVATIONS AND RESULTS

After water was added to the drawing, did the ink stay in place? Whereas after isopropyl alcohol was added, did the ink run and spread out, creating colorful artwork?

The ink used in permanent markers does not dissolve in water, meaning the ink is water insoluble. This is why when you added drops of water to the designs you made on the T-shirt, the ink should have pretty much stayed in place. Permanent marker ink, however, does dissolve in isopropyl alcohol, meaning the ink is soluble in it. Because of this, when you added drops of alcohol to the designs on the T-shirt, the ink should have spread out and ran along the fabric with the alcohol, creating a circle full of color. (This is similar to what happens when a drop of water lands on a piece of paper with something printed on it, and the ink starts to run on the paper, making the text blurry.) If you let the design that you put water drops on dry, dripping alcohol on it should make the ink run and create another colorful design on your T-shirt!

CLEANUP

Wash your hands and your work area if needed. Put away all materials used.

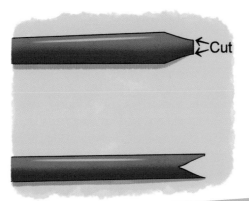

Sound Science
Do-Re-Mi with Straws

CAN YOU MAKE MUSIC WITH STRAWS? GIVE IT
A TRY IN THIS MUSICAL PROJECT.

PROJECT TIME

20 minutes

KEY CONCEPTS

Sound
Music
Physics
Sound waves
Frequency

Have you ever wondered how a musical instrument produces the beautiful sounds that it does? It all comes down to science! To make a certain note, the instrument has to generate a particular-sized sound wave. So what you hear as pitch is really just a collection of similarly sized sound waves moving through the air and hitting your ear. Of course, most instruments are capable of producing many different notes—or sizes of sound waves. Many instruments accomplish this by changing the length of part of the instrument, such as the strings in a piano or on a guitar, or a trombone's adjustable air column, or the different-length keys on a xylophone. In this science activity, you'll make your own musical instruments using drinking straws and explore how changing the length of the straws changes the notes that they produce.

45

BACKGROUND

Sound is produced by vibrations. The vibrations push and pull on air molecules, changing the air pressure around them. The pushes cause a local compression of the air (increase in pressure), and the pulls cause a local rarefaction of the air (decrease in pressure). The compressions and rarefactions are rapidly transmitted through the air from the original source as a wave, making sound. Sound itself is a wave, or a pattern, of changing air pressures.

For a sound wave, the frequency of the wave corresponds to the perceived pitch of the sound. The higher the frequency, the higher the perceived pitch. Technically, the frequency of a wave describes how many cycles of the wave happen during a certain amount of time. This is measured in hertz (Hz), which is in cycles per second. On average, the frequency range for human hearing is from 20 Hz at the low end to 20,000 Hz at the high end.

On a stringed instrument, such as a guitar or piano, when the string is plucked (guitar) or struck (piano), it vibrates and produces a standing wave on the string. These vibrations are transmitted to the soundboard of the instrument, which amplifies the sound.

MATERIALS

- At least two plastic or paper drinking straws
- Scissors
- Piano, electronic keyboard, or other musical instrument that can produce a scale of notes (optional)

PREPARATION

- Cut one of the two drinking straws so that it is half the length of the other straw. *How do you think the different lengths will affect the sounds the straws make?*

- Take one of the straws and flatten about 1 inch (2.5 cm) at one end of the straw. You can use your teeth or pinch it between your fingers or fingernails to flatten it.

- On the same straw, use scissors to make two small, angular cuts, one on each side of the flattened end. This should make the end of the straw similar to a "V" shape when flattened, but without a pointed tip at the end (the end should have a short, flat, uncut segment left).

- Repeat this with the other straw so that both have small, angular cuts on one end.

PROCEDURE

- Insert the cut end of the longer straw into your mouth. Position the cuts so they're just inside your lips. Then curve your lips down and inward a little and apply light pressure on the straw with your lips. *Why do you think you need to apply pressure to the straw?*

- Blow through the straw. *What do you hear?* The cut ends should vibrate and produce a tone. You may need to move the straw around slightly to locate the best position for creating your musical note. It might take some practice and repeated tries to produce a constant, single note.

- Now blow through the shorter straw using the same method. *What do you hear this time? How does it compare to what you heard with the longer straw?* Again, you might need to try blowing through the straw a few times to make it produce a constant, single note.

ExTRA

If you have a piano, electronic keyboard, or other kind of musical instrument, you could try comparing the notes from the straws to the notes on the real musical instrument. *Can you figure out which notes the straws are making? Can you tell what the relationship is between the two notes? How does the note from the shorter straw compare to the note from the longer straw?*

EXTRA ～～～～～～～～～～～～～～～～～～～～

You could try repeating this activity, but use eight straws and try to cut them so that each straw produces a note from a scale. For example, for a scale starting with C, these eight notes correspond to the white keys on a piano: C, D, E, F, G, A, B, C. *Can you make a scale using eight straws cut to different lengths?*

EXTRA ～～～～～～～～～～～～～～～～～～～～

Other instruments are easy to make as well! You can make multiple notes by filling soda bottles with different amounts of water and blowing across the tops of them (see the activity on p. 30), or by filling goblets with different amounts of water and using a clean, slightly wet finger to stroke around the rim of the glass to cause vibrations. *How do the notes produced by these instruments change when you change how much water is in them? Can you use them to play a scale or a song?*

OBSERVATIONS AND RESULTS ·············

Did the shorter straw play a much higher-pitched sound than the longer straw?

The pitch of a sound corresponds to the frequency of the sound wave. The higher the frequency, the higher the perceived pitch. The shorter straw should have made a sound wave with a higher frequency than the longer straw, and so the shorter straw should have made a higher pitch than the longer straw.

In fact, because the shorter straw was half the length of the longer straw, the shorter straw should have produced a frequency that was twice the longer straw's frequency. (This is based on a mathematical equation that describes how the frequency produced in an open cylinder is affected by the cylinder's length, where the frequency equals the velocity of sound—which should be constant—divided by two times the cylinder's length.) When one sound wave is twice the frequency of another sound wave, the pitches are one octave apart. For example, the musical note Middle C has a frequency of 262 Hz, and the C note one octave above this has a frequency of 524 Hz (or two times 262 Hz). However, you may have found that it can take some practice using the straw instruments in this activity to produce a constant, single note.

CLEANUP ··

Throw out your used straws. Put away any other materials you used.

Seeing Science
Why Do Video Game Characters Look Better Now?

IT'S TIME TO GET CREATIVE AND EXPLORE HOW AN INCREASED NUMBER OF PIXELS CAN MAKE VIDEO GAME ART AND CHARACTERS LOOK EVEN BETTER!

Have you ever wondered why video games today look better than the ones from the 1980s? Today we have video games with relatively realistic figures, a lot of color, and a lot of details—but these were not features of games from four decades ago. One major change between then and now is the number of pixels, or dots on the screen, used to represent video game objects. In this science activity, you will put your artistic talent to use and investigate how increasing the number of pixels might make a video game character look better.

PROJECT TIME

1 hour

KEY CONCEPTS

Computers
Pictures
Resolution
Technology
Data

49

BACKGROUND

Pixels are the smallest unit of data in a digital picture. If you were able to magnify your TV screen or computer monitor many times, you'd see that the entire screen is arranged with thousands of small dots or squares, like a piece of graph paper. Each dot or square is a pixel. To make a picture, each pixel is filled in with a single color and many pixels are placed next to one another to form an image.

The first home video game consoles, like the Nintendo Entertainment System (NES), couldn't store or display much data, so not that many pixels could be shown on the screen at a time. Because of this, the video game characters and other video game art used far fewer pixels. But today's video game consoles can store much more data, so the characters are higher resolution. When Nintendo first introduced the Super Mario Bros. game for its NES in 1985, Mario was only 16 by 12 pixels in size. Decades later, the Mario character in Super Paper Mario Wii is composed of more than 17 times as many pixels. (He's 67 by 50 pixels!)

MATERIALS

- Computer with internet access and a printer
- Two different pages of custom graph paper (You can print it from a free graph paper website or you can draw your own graph paper using a ruler, pen or pencil, and two sheets of paper.)
- Pen or pencil
- Ruler
- Colored pencils, crayons, or markers

PREPARATION

- If you want to draw your own graph paper (instead of printing it), on one sheet of paper make a grid with lines that are about a 1/4 inch (6 mm) apart. Make the grid 33 by 33 lines this way. On a second sheet of paper, make a grid with lines that are about 3/4 inch (19 mm) apart. Make this grid 9 by 9 lines.

50

- If you use a free graph paper website, make and print a sheet of graph paper with "grid spacing" of five lines per 1 inch (2.5 cm). Then make and print a second piece of graph paper that is 1.25 lines per 1 inch (2.5 cm).

- Using a ruler and a pen or pencil, draw a box on the first piece of graph paper (the one with more squares) that is 32 by 32 squares. Each square will represent a single pixel, so there will be a total of 1,024 pixels within the box.

- Similarly, draw a box on the second piece of graph paper that is 8 by 8 squares. There will be a total of 64 pixels within this box, which should be about the same size as the box on the other sheet of paper.

PROCEDURE

- With colored pencils, crayons, or markers, draw a character inside the 32 by 32-pixel box you made. The character can be any character you want. You can draw something from your own imagination or try to copy an existing character. Add as much detail as possible to your character, but each pixel can only contain a single color (and must be completely colored in). The character does not have to take up all 1,024 pixels (you can leave some blank), but it should reach just about to each side of the big box you have drawn. *How does your character look when you finish?*

- Using the colored pencils or other drawing tools, draw your character again, but this time in the 8 by 8-pixel box on the other sheet of graph paper. Draw the same character as you did before, trying to keep as many of the details the same between the two drawings. But again, only one color can be used per square, and each square must be entirely filled in. *How does the character look on this sheet of paper? How was it to draw the character in this version?*

Compare the high-resolution (32 by 32-pixel) drawing of the character with the low-resolution (8 by 8-pixel) drawing of the same character. *Which drawing has more detail? Which drawing looks more realistic?*

ExTRA

You can repeat this activity a few more times, but draw other characters, monsters, or objects. *Are your results always the same?*

ExTRA

Try this activity again in the finer grid, but this time add additional drawings of the character at resolutions of 64 by 64 pixels and 128 by 128 pixels (but keep the overall drawing size the same). *How does adding even more pixels affect the level of detail in your picture?*

ExTRA

Compare the minimum number of pixels it takes to make different shapes. Some shapes you can try are triangles, diamonds, stars, circles, and hexagons. *Are certain shapes easier than others to make using just a few pixels?*

OBSERVATIONS AND RESULTS ··········

Did the character in the higher-resolution box (32 by 32 pixels) have more detail and overall look more realistic than the character in the lower-resolution box (8 by 8 pixels)?

Resolution refers to how many pixels wide and high an image is. Generally, the higher resolution an image is (the more pixels it contains) the more detail we can see and the more realistic it looks to us. The character you drew in the 32 by 32-pixel box has more pixels (1,024) compared with the character in the 8 by 8-pixel box (which contained 64), but they should both take up about the same amount of space (because the pixels in the 32 by 32 box were much smaller than the ones in the 8 by 8 box).

Specifically, when trying to draw the same character in the 8 by 8-pixel box you may have found it was difficult to maintain many of the details from when you drew it in the 32 by 32-pixel box, and you had to make tough decisions about which details to include and how to show them without completely distorting the image.

CLEANUP ·

If you like your drawings, hang them up to show your family and friends! Otherwise, recycle your used paper and put away all other materials used.

Staining Science
Make the Boldest, Brightest Dye!

DOES FABRIC MATTER WHEN USING DYE? FIND OUT
IN THIS COLORFUL EXPERIMENT!

Have you ever wondered about the materials that make up your clothes and why some look and feel different from others? The clothes you wear are made of fibers that come from many different sources. Some fabrics are made from natural fibers and others are from manufactured, or totally synthetic, fibers. In this activity, you'll explore how well different fiber types can be dyed using fiber-reactive dye. Aren't you just dye-ing to find out which fabric works best?

PROJECT TIME
4 hours

KEY CONCEPTS
Chemistry
Dyes
Fabric

54

BACKGROUND

From woven mummy shrouds in ancient Egypt to the ornate ball gowns ladies wore in the Victorian era to the tie-dyed shirts that gained popularity in the 1970s, dyed cloth has played an important role in human culture. Its production has also changed over time. Early dyes were made using natural resources, like plants, berries, minerals, and seeds. The cloths, just like the dyes, were made from a natural resource—such as cotton, linen, wool, or silk. Cotton and linen fibers are all formed from cellulose, the main component of plant cell walls. Wool and silk are fibers that are animal protein based.

Later, as advancements were made in chemistry and manufacturing, people learned to make other fibers, including polyester, nylon, and rayon, which are known as synthetic fibers. Today's dyes are also different—they are now often made with artificial chemicals. By understanding how the molecules of dye react with the different types of fibers, chemists can design many vibrant and color-fast dyes (which means that they won't fade or run) and figure out on which fiber types they work best.

MATERIALS

- Three different types of white fabric samples: such as linen, cotton-polyester blend, 100 percent polyester, 100 percent cotton, wool, rayon, silk, or nylon. Collect enough to make at least one 10-inch by 10-inch (25 cm by 25 cm) square of each type. Preferably select one natural fabric, a synthetic one, and one that is a blend of both. Scraps from old pillow cases, sheets, rags, or unwanted clothes can make good sources—just be sure they are okay for you to use and that you know the fabric type. Otherwise, small pieces can be purchased from a craft or fabric store.
- Ruler
- Scissors
- Permanent marker
- Newspaper or rags
- Measuring cup, which will not be used for cooking afterward (If unavailable, create a discardable plastic cup measurer. To do this, measure out 1/2 cup [118 ml]

of water, pour it in the disposable cup and mark the top of the water with a permanent marker. Dump out the water and repeat with 1 cup [236 ml] of water. Use this marked container as your measuring cup.)

Laundry detergent

Safety goggles or protective glasses

Rubber gloves

Clean glass jar, at least 10 fluid ounces (295 ml). It should not be used to consume food or beverages afterward.

Measuring teaspoon and tablespoon. (They should not be used for cooking afterward. If unavailable, measure 1 teaspoon [5 ml] of water into a disposable plastic spoon and note the quantity. Repeat with 1 tablespoon [15 ml].)

Fiber-reactive dye powder, such as Tulip Permanent Fabric Dye or Procion Pro MX Reactive Dye, often available at a craft and/or fabric store. Use a bold color, like red, blue or green.

Salt

Water

Sealable plastic bag, one-gallon size

Timer or clock

Soda ash or Arm & Hammer Super Washing Soda

Plastic container that can hold 4 cups (946 ml) comfortably. (It should not be used for food or beverage afterward.)

Old clothes to wear that can get stained

PREPARATION ·······························

● Cut at least one 10-inch by 10-inch (25 cm by 25 cm) square out of each fabric sample (linen, cotton-polyester, and 100 percent polyester, for example).

- Use the permanent marker to label each square with its fabric type. Because the permanent marker may leak through some types of fabric, if you are not working on a surface that can be stained, label the fabrics on top of newspaper or rags.

- Prewash the fabric squares by putting them in a normal clothes washing machine with laundry detergent. Wash using hot water, if possible. Allow the fabric squares to air dry.

- Before opening the dye powder packet, cover the area you will be working on with newspaper or rags so that you will not stain it. You might want to work outside to avoid staining something. Also put on clothes that you would not mind staining.

- Dyes often contain soda ash (sodium carbonate), which is caustic. Wear goggles and gloves when mixing the dye solution, mixing the soda ash solution, and rinsing the fabric samples after dyeing.

PROCEDURE

- Put on gloves and safety goggles.

- Put 2 teaspoons of powdered dye, 1 tablespoon of salt, and 1 cup (236 ml) of warm water into the glass jar. Mix thoroughly. *How does the dye look?*

- Wet the fabric squares with water and place them in the sealable plastic bag. Carefully pour the dye solution into the bag then add 1/2 cup (118 ml) of water. Seal the bag, trapping as little air as possible. *How does the fabric change when the dye is added?*

- Let the bag sit for 20 minutes. Every couple of minutes, gently squeeze the bag to coat all of the fabric samples.

- While the fabric is soaking, mix 1 tablespoon of soda ash (or Arm & Hammer Super Washing Soda) with 2 cups (473 ml) of warm water in the plastic container. Break up any hard pieces that form.

57

After the fabric is done soaking, carefully open the plastic bag and add 1/2 cup (118 ml) of the soda ash solution. Reseal the bag, trapping as little air as possible.

Gently squeeze the bag to mix the soda ash, dye, and fabric. Let the bag sit for one hour, gently squeezing every 10 minutes or so.

With gloved hands, reach into the bag and retrieve the fabric samples and place them on a surface where they will not stain anything. Carefully dump the contents of the bag into a sink (pouring directly into the drain so as not to stain any of the sink area).

Rinse the fabric until the water runs clear. When you are done handling the rinsed fabric and disposing of the soda ash solution, you can remove your goggles and gloves. Wash the fabric samples in the washing machine just as you did before (but not with any other clothes). Allow the samples to air dry.

Once they're dry, how do the fabric samples look? Did some types of fabric become dyed to a darker shade than others? Did some types not absorb much dye at all?

⚛ SCIENCE FAIR IDEA 〜〜〜

In this activity, you tested how well different fabric samples dyed using a fiber-reactive dye. But there are many other types of fabric you could test dyeing, and they may react differently. *How well do other types of fabric become dyed with a fiber-reactive dye?*

SCIENCE FAIR IDEA

Before synthetic dyes were created, humans used natural dyes. Do some background research and pick one or more natural dyes to try in this activity. You will probably want to use relatively safe dyes, such as turmeric or berries. Be just as careful with these around other surfaces and materials, as they also stain easily. *Do some natural dyes work better than others? Does it depend on the type of fabric used?*

OBSERVATIONS AND RESULTS ·········

Did coarse, natural fabrics, such as linen or 100 percent cotton, become dyed the darkest shade? Did synthetic fabrics, such as polyester or rayon, remain nearly white? Did fabrics that were a blend of natural and synthetic fibers become noticeably dyed, but not quite as dark as fully natural fabrics?

Cotton and linen fibers are both natural fibers made from cellulose, a compound found in plant cell walls. Fiber-reactive dyes form permanent covalent chemical bonds with cellulose, making this dyeing process a relatively permanent one. Polyester, however, is a synthetic fiber that does not react with fiber-reactive dyes in this way and cannot be effectively dyed using them. For polyester to be successfully dyed, a different category of dyes must be used—specifically dispersion dyes, and a great deal of heat has to be applied during the dyeing process. In this activity you probably saw that synthetic fabrics were not effectively dyed, remaining nearly white, whereas the natural fabrics dyed the darkest shade, and the blend fabrics were not quite as dark as the natural fabric (depending on the percentage of natural and synthetic fibers in the fabric).

CLEANUP ·······································

You can safely pour the extra soda ash solution down the drain, flushing with water. Do not use the measuring cup, measuring spoons, plastic container, or glass jar for cooking or food afterward. Carefully rinse and then recycle the plastic sealable bag.

THE SCIENTIFIC METHOD

The scientific method helps scientists—and students—gather facts to prove whether an idea is true. Using this method, scientists come up with ideas and then test those ideas by observing facts and drawing conclusions. You can use the scientific method to develop and test your own ideas!

Question: What do you want to learn? What problem needs to be solved? Be as specific as possible.

Research: Learn more about your topic and refine your question.

Hypothesis: Form an educated guess about what you think will answer your question. This allows you to make a prediction you can test.

Experiment: Create a test to learn if your hypothesis is correct. Limit the number of variables, or elements of the experiment that could change.

Analysis: Record your observations about the progress and results of your experiment. Then analyze your data to understand what it means.

Conclusion: Review all your data. Did the results of the experiment match the prediction? If so, your hypothesis was correct. If not, your hypothesis may need to be changed.

GLOSSARY

composition: The way a thing, like a photograph, is put together or arranged.

compression: The act of pressing or squeezing together.

equidistant: An equal distance.

extract: To draw matter out of something by using a machine or chemicals.

minerals: Matter in the ground that makes up rocks.

penetrate: To pass into something.

pitch: How high or low a sound is.

prediction: A guess made based on facts or knowledge.

represent: To stand for something else.

resonant: Having to do with causing resonance, or the increased musical tone created by vibration.

solvent: The liquid used to dissolve another substance.

surfactant: Matter that acts on the surface, such as a laundry detergent.

technique: A certain way of doing something.

toxic: Having to do with being poisonous or harmful to the body.

versatile: Having many uses.

ADDITIONAL RESOURCES

Books

Jacoby, Jenny. *The Illustrated Encyclopedia of STEAM Words: An A to Z of 100 Terms Kids Need To Know!* New York, NY: Racehorse for Young Readers, 2022.

Olson, Elsie. *Get Messy with Science!: Projects that Ooze, Foam, and More.* North Mankato, MN: Capstone Press, 2023.

Welker, Liz, and Sam Spendlove. *DIY Guide to Tie Dye Style: The Basics & Way Beyond.* Lafayette, CA: Stash Books, 2021.

Websites

Discovery Education
sciencefaircentral.com

Exploratorium
www.exploratorium.edu/search/science%20fair%20projects

Science Buddies
www.sciencebuddies.org/science-fair-projects/project-ideas/list

Science Fun for Everyone!
www.sciencefun.org/?s=science+fair

Videos

Recycled Material Art | Arts InSight
https://ny.pbslearningmedia.org/resource/recycled-material-art-video/arts-insight/

Test the Scientific Method Against This Card Trick | Camp TV
https://ny.pbslearningmedia.org/resource/ctv21-test-the-scientific-method-video/camp-tv/

What Is Music? | Music Arts Toolkit
https://ny.pbslearningmedia.org/resource/ket-music-basics-overview-101/what-is-music-music-arts-toolkit/

INDEX